LET'S

One woman's spiritual quest for answers about the meaning of Life; that began with a death, ended with a death, then started again with Love.

Pamela Lind

Let's Go Home

By Pamela Lind

Cover Design by Pamela Lind

Artwork by Pamela Lind

ISBN: 978-1-7366006-1-0

Contents

Acknowledgments

It would not feel right to proceed without offering my humble gratitude to all entities, visible and invisible, for the countless gifts that have brought me to the peace and fulfillment I had always craved.

I left out the names of people and places because the focus is on the experiences themselves. Those experiences were specifically tailored for me as I continued to pursue my ultimate desire to understand. You will have your own.

Also, I especially want to thank those who took the time out of their busy lives to assist me in the process of putting it all together into this book.

And for the readers—thank you for being here with me.

Prologue

"We do not write in order to be understood; we write to understand."

Cecil Day-Lewis

This isn't a story about my personal life regarding the many painful situations that have made their weave upon life's tapestry. We all have had those situations arise and, for the most part, endured somehow. Instead, the focus is what I found to be available experientially, bringing about peace of mind and, at times, total freedom or bliss.

I write this journal of sorts to organize some of the highlights that came out of the many experiences that still shine in the folds of my memory. It seemed important to do this, probably more for me than anyone else. But maybe, just maybe, it will be inspiring to others.

These experiences started to flow my way as soon as I asked the question—"Why?" Why are we here? Why do we get sick and or die? Why is happiness so fleeting? You know—the usual. I only had to learn how to listen and to trust—for forty years plus. Well, I have my answers, and then some. But I am still listening to the Voice that is always present within.

I realize that some will judge the following material, but that is the way of being human. It doesn't matter. I can take a stand for what I believe because of these experiences, for they removed the blocks to Love's presence. I found that this Love is indeed our natural inheritance from our Creator.

It says, in *A Course In Miracles*, "A universal theology is impossible, but a universal experience is not only possible but necessary."

The way I see it, having your own experience is the only way to know the Truth...if you want!

Here are some of mine.

Smoke and Mirrors

I had a vision, of sorts, during a writing retreat. I could see a horrific battle being fought—as my present surroundings wholly disappeared. I could tell it was a war that seemed to have been going on forever and ever; the reason for fighting hardly known anymore. It was down to simple survival!

My focus was on two men, in particular, that were going at it with all the rage and hatred humanly possible. Both were pretty much equal in the number of bleeding wounds. It was only the grip of dark determination for what they vaguely remembered as their truth or purpose and the fear of losing that kept them standing and fighting.

One warrior was just about to give the fatal blow when— *something extraordinary happened.*

Instantly, all the fighting stopped! I could not hear or see anything to be the cause!

It was as though a switch had been flipped, and all the hatred disappeared. As far as the eye could see, all the soldiers who had fallen, either injured or dead, were getting up and dusting themselves off.

Then they all vanished.

∞

As I watched that scene play out in my mind, I knew right then and there; I had had an epiphany! I had been shown a revelation so profound that it actually made me laugh outright.

9

"I get it!" I whispered as the effects of this experience moved throughout my system, changing my perceptions of our world—forever.

Just 40 years earlier...

The Shock

He's dead.

I felt so numb I couldn't even begin to make sense of it all. I mean, I just saw him that morning! Like a zombie, I undressed and entered the shower, keeping the water as hot as I could stand it. I buried my face into the far corner of the stall, and I began to sob silently—body heaving with each why, why, why.

As I tried to reassemble the fragments of my shattered mind—no, it felt like my very *soul*—I reflected on an earlier time when he was still alive. I figure if I coax my mind to inch forward slowly, very slowly, image by image, surely, I will be able to figure something out—anything!

What did I miss?

∞

The blankety-blank alarm clock was going off. Geez, I really hate those things! I don't need one. I can tell myself what time I need to wake up, and voila, I do. Only this wasn't for me, and I wasn't sure my inner clock would work for him.

After the cacophony stopped, I could hear the rain pounding outside. So much for southern California's sunny skies! LA traffic was going to be a nightmare, and his commute would be even further—from my place.

He literally leaped out of bed and seemingly, straight into his clothes. How did he do that? "See ya," he said. "I'll give you a call later."

I opened one eye and mumbled, "Be careful. It's raining like crazy."

He leaned over me and tousled my hair. "Hey honey, you don't have to worry about me." Then off he went, and I—back to sleep.

Now, were we in love? I honestly couldn't answer that question. There were strong feelings—yes. But we were young, just enjoying each other's company and not thinking too far ahead into the future. Besides, what is love anyway? I mean, really!

He called when he got home from work and reminded me about his 'game' that evening. It was a local men's softball league or some such. And for reasons unknown, at the time, I decided to sit this one out. If he were up for it, though, I would throw some dinner together, and he could come over afterward. Sounded like a plan, we agreed, and that was that.

I waited and waited while aimlessly flipping through the only TV channels that were available back then in 1978. I was still waiting, moving past boredom, and starting to get angry. The least he could do is call if something else came up!

I jump, startled, as finally, the phone rings. The piercing noise is almost as bad as the alarm clock, but it's not him. It's the girlfriend of his best buddy, and she's acting hysterical, saying, "...he just died, and they took him in an ambulance to the closest hospital and on and on and on..." And I am no longer listening. For it is simply not true.

I must have hung up at some point. In a daze, I called my mother, who lived fairly close by, and shared the strange news.

"Just in case it's true, maybe I should go over to the hospital to check things out," I say with a voice that sounded from somewhere far, far away.

"Nope! No, no, no. Not a good idea; going by yourself. We will come and get you," I hear her familiar voice say within the dense fog that had now enveloped me.

"Oooo kaaay. I'lll get reaadeee," I barely manage in response.

I don't recall anything of that process, purse, locking the door, and all that; until I find myself waiting on the curb in darkness. I'm picked up, and all the familiar landscape along the way was just a blur. We pull into the parking area close to the emergency entrance, and before the car stops, I open the door and jump out in a full run, entering the building. It is a very small waiting area, and I see familiar faces; his best buddy and, oh jeez, his Mom, which is not a good sign. But I need proof, with my own eyes!

Someone says something to a nurse, and she ushers me into a very plain, tiny room. It seems small anyway, minuscule even, with a gurney to one side. On it, a body covered with a drape. "Do you want to see him?" she asks.

"No, oh no," I gasp. She left the room as I sank to my knees. I did reach over to touch his hand that had escaped the sheet and dangled down toward me. It was still warm. I don't think I passed out, but I must have simply blanked out, for I have no memory of anything or anyone who later said that they had come in to comfort me. At some point, I finally did feel a hand on my shoulder and the words, "He's gone. It was his heart. Let's go. There's nothing you can do now."

However, later in the shower, I vow to get answers to the why of it all. We only have one life to live.

His ended at twenty-six!

The Quest: Metaphysical This And That

In just a short few months after the funeral, I had my first adventure into the unknown territory of the invisible, mystical world—which, I might add, ended up being quite bizarre!

At this point, my Christian upbringing wasn't helping me out at all. Grandma had paved the way for my early experiences of Jesus, for she loved Him with great abandon. And that had had a calming influence in those younger years. In fact, I had my first experience of unconditional love through her.

So, I loved Jesus too and talked to Him easily as a friend—quite a lot actually, as only an innocent child could. But somehow, as time went by, I drifted and drifted some more until I could no longer truly connect with the message of Christianity or its Messenger—especially after *The Shock*. Plus, the church had way too many rules. So, my life proceeded to take a seemingly radical turn, spiritually.

I was asking just about everybody I came in contact with, their belief on why we are here, and where do we go after we die, and so forth and so on. So, when someone was willing to introduce me to a different kind of message, under very different circumstances, I was game. The message was about love and joy and the God *within*. That was new news to me—the God within part. But the circumstances were somewhat distracting. It was a gathering of followers of a very beloved teacher who had died. Tapes had been made of that person (while living, of course), channeling another entity (in spirit form), whose messages were still of great interest to said people and continue to be played. Okay...

Through all these years, what stayed with me was that I could smell the heavy scent of roses on the way out. As I looked around, I saw a bouquet sitting on a side table near the entrance. I approached and bent to get a deeper whiff. My eyes flew open when my nose came in contact with not dewy petals but hard plastic! Dusty plastic, I might add!

"What's the deal here? I can actually smell roses in this area!" I whispered to the person that brought me. It was explained that the bouquet sitting there was symbolic because this particular 'spirit' always carried roses. Hmmm...

I have to say that with all things considered, I wondered why this whole, extraordinary experience—my very first one to boot—felt somewhat natural to me. I was raised to believe that it was most certainly the work of the devil! Could it be that I was uncovering an aspect of reality or truth that I somehow already knew?

I kept moving forward with my search.

∞

I was with another group, an ESP weekend workshop, I believe, when the teacher paused and told us that she was now going to ask a certain 'spirit' to appear and shower us with light. Well, that got my attention! Smelling invisible roses offered by a spirit was one thing but seeing an invisible someone would be off the charts! But I looked and looked and couldn't see a thing. Disappointed and getting a little bored, I began to drift off and shift into daydream mode when suddenly, I was surprised by an image of a robed being that appeared right next to the teacher! I saw a vague outline of hands with fingers pointing up and palms open, reaching out towards us, all bathed in bright, amber light.

The light within the hooded part of the robe was so bright that I could not see any facial features. Yikes! This all happened in a split second or two. But when it dawned on me that I was actually seeing a spirit or something to that effect, my physical eyes took over, and the image disappeared. I tried to replicate my experience, tried being the keyword here, but I couldn't do it.

∞

I attended another workshop dealing with altered states of consciousness and psychic abilities with yet a different teacher. Two things stand out here. One, we had a spoon-bending session in which I saw many attendees hold up their spoons and rub with their thumbs, right below the rounded portion or bowl. This was a *mind over matter* demonstration, and I literally saw spoons bending down in a graceful flow with my eyes this time. It was happening left and right except, of course—in my own hand!

Later, we gathered in small groups and handed the assistant a piece of paper on which we had previously written the name, age, and city of residence of someone we knew that had an illness or condition of some sort. This task was to be an 'absentee scan and healing' exercise. Next, we were handed one of those slips of paper (not ours, of course) and proceeded to go through the process of relaxing and opening up to a total stranger, that was represented only by a scant few facts on a piece of paper.

I forgot the relaxing and opening part and went headlong into trying—once more. I was on a mission! So, I fussed and mussed around until being the last one to have any kind of experience at all, the assistant finally says, "Just envision the person's head on your shoulders! Be that person."

Ooooh, that's weird, I thought, but I did just that. And lo and behold, in my mind's eye, I couldn't see a thing except for a tiny bit of extremely vague light in all the darkness! I shared what had occurred for me with the group, and the student who knew my 'subject' personally, said that he was blind! That was a very emotional moment for me as the tears began to flow. How was that even possible?

∞

I had my first healing experience. That was what they called it, but others might say it was a 'laying on of hands' session. I arrived feeling unsure about some decisions I needed to make and was feeling alternately anxious then depressed. Not long after the session began, the tension simply faded away. The relaxation was much like one would get with a massage, but without any physical manipulation. I could actually feel movement or energy coursing through my body! I decided to book several sessions to see if it would happen again. Each time I arrived in various states of emotional or mental disarray, and each time I left in a peaceful state. I just couldn't hold that state for very long. So now I began to wonder if I could learn to do this for myself and others.

Many classes, workshops, and an internship later (about four years), I graduated from this healing center, which was also a church, with a bachelor's degree in Natural Theology and at the same time, was ordained as a Minister of Healing. Being ordained gave me a platform from which I could lay hands on people legally. There is power in the touch, especially when Divinity is invited. You know the saying… "When two or more are gathered in My Name…"

Speaking of which, one experience stood out where I was working on someone, and when finished, I asked, as always, what was their experience. It was the one time when during the session that a person felt a second pair of hands along with mine. This, coming from an engineer! Now, I'm not saying who showed up and helped that day, but it was a very exciting confirmation.

It was hard to build a practice that could support me financially. Even though I had very positive feedback, I didn't dare quit my business. After all the effort involved—I simply wasn't confident enough in myself or had the faith necessary to support this endeavor in the long run.

∞

Still searching…

I heard it first from a Tibetan monk—that Satan is the ego. That made a lot of sense to me!

I attended sweat lodges and Vision Quests honoring all cultures. It was LA, after all! And I also looked into the past life therapy—quite a bit, in fact. All very interesting!

There was an adult education school not far from where I lived, and I took my first painting class in watercolor. Enjoyed it, but…

Also, I took another class there that taught the basic concepts written in the books called *A Course In Miracles* and bought the set. I started to study them, but I just couldn't wrap my mind around what I was reading. Those concepts just flew right over me!

So, like a butterfly, I went from flower to flower, or teaching to teaching, and drank from each, their nectar of truth, learning from all the different sources I was attracted to. But when would the actual transformation of Self-realization that was being taught occur? When would I feel that my questions about life were answered?

I paused, looked up from all that going and doing, and noticed that twelve years had passed. And what did I have to show for it? A massive library of metaphysical, spiritual, religious, self-help books on just about every perception out there. I had completed numerous workshops, seminars, and educational programs, most with certificates. So what! Big deal! I had spent probably thousands of dollars towards my quest, and oh, you can even throw in visits to a psychic and a shrink or two!

I still felt blind, or that something was missing as I groped around for the one experience or the 'ah-ha' that would fulfill me. Life continued to be a seesaw of emotions, yet I still felt a subtle force guiding me forward.

∞

Oh, and one more...

The roads were wet and slippery from the pouring rain during the early hours that morning, which is typical of the tropics. We were late for a diving excursion offered on the other side of the island. We thought of canceling due to the weather but at the last moment decided to take the risk.

I held on tight in the passenger seat and ducked my head a bit as we took a turn way too fast. The tires lost their grip. It was a very long slide as time went into slow motion. I had begun to duck even more because we were in a convertible jeep when I felt an arm around my shoulders, holding me tight. After the vehicle came to a halt, I raised my head and saw that we were okay, just stuck in the mud on the opposite side of the road going in the wrong direction. Once unstuck and on our way again, I was feeling very grateful—very grateful indeed. For the early morning hours with hardly any traffic, and for the physical support I felt.

"Thanks so much for putting your arm around me. I was really terrified!" I exclaimed.

"Are you nuts? I had to keep both hands on the wheel just to try to keep the jeep from flipping over, he says!"

Oh...I thought. Now, I have felt spirit! Why me, or does this occur often to others?

The Abyss

I was married by now to a four-year, sober alcoholic and addict that I had met during another seminar. For the life of me, I don't remember what the attraction was. Still, some part of me was moved in his direction. As I recall, he had an air of confidence about him, which, I later realized, covered a multitude of issues that I simply ignored. That confidence was something I wanted for myself. So maybe that was it—because I do believe that opposites attract, and for good reason!

Plus, I figured that two people on a spiritual path could overcome anything! But it was my naiveté, need to be loved, and persistent battle with depression, mixed with his smooth-talking (lying), money issues, and values that didn't fly with me; that spelled disaster and created a living nightmare for us both.

I eventually lost my house and everything I had worked so hard for. But before that happened...

∞

I was leafing through the mail and noticed an envelope addressed to me. It looked very much like the usual junk (at least it wasn't another bill), so instead of tossing it, I decided to give it a look. At first glance, the message communicated definitely piqued my interest. Even though I couldn't put my finger on what exactly, it seemed somewhat different from my past search, since *The Shock*. So, I made a call to check it out.

This group was offering an intro evening into the energy process that they used. Since it was a must that one commits to their basic nine-month program, I needed to know more. I called and spoke with a woman who seemed quite nice, loving even, and very down to earth. Because of her, I registered to attend. Little did I know that the woman I had just spoken with would later become a friend beyond compare—a 'soul sister' of like mind.

I fight the Friday night traffic and spend almost two hours with the members and those, like me, who might be interested. However, by the end of the evening, I still did not have a clue as to what was being offered. But I did sign up for the next step. Some invisible force kept urging me forward.

Next was the interview process, which was much more personal and intimate. It was a must for all parties to be sure that the choice to become a member was the right one! That, in and of itself, was fascinating. I mean, who cares! You have a message or technique to help one acquire peace or whatever, and you share it! Why all the intrigue?

∞

I arrive at their office, which was in a small apartment complex and had a good homey vibe. Two female members were already waiting for me—one of which I had initially talked to and liked right off—you know, the soul sister.

The interview was to be a 'view between' the three of us to see if this program was my next step. Now I am going into much more detail than all the other group experiences I've had because I was very literally about to take a huge leap forward. In comparison, it would be like driving one of the first Volkswagens to make your journey, versus a spaceship!

It seemed like the two women were meditating or something—so we are sitting there in silence. That silence goes on and on and on. It started to get on my nerves! I began to ask questions like, "Well...what exactly do you do here?"

Their answer seemed oblique and had none of the specifics I was looking for. I decided to list all the things I had done, blah, blah, blah. I was feeling pretty smug about all of it too! I mean, what could they possibly have to offer, over and above all of what I have experienced? Aside from the fact that it was me who wanted in!

They proceeded to tell me that we would have a 'shared experience' and know 'it' if and when 'it' happened. Two hours had passed, and nothing remarkable had occurred. By now, it was clear that they were ready to call it quits.

Something was mentioned about some resistance on my part! What? That was a first! Obviously, something wasn't happening here, but it most certainly wasn't because of me!

We all looked at each other, and I saw they were seriously going to wrap up our little session. I started to panic. I felt like a deer in headlights! It seemed like they knew something I didn't. Then I found myself saying, "I really, truly, want to get this!" as the tears began to roll down my cheeks. Right then and there—BOOM—I have a vision. I saw this dark, armor, or wall-like barrier in front of me, closing me off completely from what—I did not know. This barrier cracked open ever so slightly, and the brightest light came into my system like a healing balm replacing fears which had ruled in the form of extreme arrogance only a moment ago. That was my first Vision, except when I saw the entity of light all those years ago!

That was...that was...incredible! I couldn't speak for some time, but the two women knew that something profound had happened to me. They said that they could feel it in their hearts and that I looked different.

I was so grateful for their patience and loving embrace while I stood in such total defiance. Pleased that 'it' had finally happened, we all hugged and said goodbye. I still didn't know what lay ahead, but if it was anything like what had occurred that night—I was ready for more.

Well, sort of...because as the light from that experience was already starting to dim, doubt took its place. Is nothing ever permanent?

∞

As their nine-month program began, I found myself with at least half a dozen other students and two teachers. We met for a couple of hours or so once a week and tried to learn the difference between speaking from the heart versus the head and from feelings rather than emotions. Oh, and be present also!

I became painfully aware of how insecure I truly was and how hard I worked to cover all that up. This process was like a laser that cuts through all pretenses and brought me in direct contact with something else entirely—when I let go. It was like the interview all over again, and again, and again. I was terrified and wanted to quit several times. But, recognizing that I would be failing myself, I hung in there.

The payoff from each breakthrough, no matter how small, was a feeling of exhilaration that made me hunger for more.

∞

There was a weekend intensive for all the students. It was time to go all the way and blast through the debris of darkness and chaos, that is the ego, and reveal the true self deep inside. But we didn't know that! It started out business-as-usual, sitting quietly within an embrace of loving energy we called the 'active component' of God.

Some people were sitting in chairs, some on the floor and others, simply laid down, where there was room. Again, not a lot was going on that was apparent.

I, myself, eventually got to the point where it seemed as though I was standing at the precipice of an abyss. The depth and darkness were unfathomable. I was terrified to the point of immobility. If I proceeded, I would surely die. No ifs, ands, or buts about it!

The facilitators were going around to each person to assist in any way that would lessen the grip of fear during the process. Why was this so hard? It would be laughable if I could stand back and see myself sitting there with no gun to my head, not even a cruel word—just love, straight from the heart.

Upon being stressed to the maximum, I decided not to quit as was the norm for me but take a leap of faith. If others could let go and have this experience (whatever it was going to be), then I could too.

In my mind's eye, I jumped...

But instead of falling into the pitch black of the unknown, I stepped off into the most loving space of light beyond imagination.

Wha... I was speechless.

There was no way to ever know before this moment that I was so embraced and so loved. The tears coursed down my face. I could not contain my feelings. I wanted to sing, dance, and lovingly caress everyone around me. Yes, this was Heaven. I had experienced something I had always yearned for—but never made the connection.

I continued to bask in the essence of that glorious experience with a smile from ear to ear. After a while, once I began to settle back into myself from that expanded state, I was asked to help others who were still stuck. It was heartbreaking to see them struggle—some simply left the building. We lost a few members that weekend. They just couldn't or wouldn't take the final step. The ego had won again.

This sacred place seemed to be deep within my heart and felt like a gateway of sorts into—well, the only way I can honestly say this without speculating, is a place free of the ego's grip. That was what I had only a glimpse of at the end of my initial interview. We called it the 'shared place,' and it is in all of us, uniting us. This I know for certain. It is a place of complete, unfettered honesty and goes beyond any physicality into the domain of Love and the absolute knowing that we are all One.

∞

After the nine-month program was complete, all of the members came together with us graduates at a meet and greet retreat. Of course, it was so much more. I remember during a long, silent reflection, I became aware of a figure in front of me. This entity did not show itself as human but rather as a smoky shadow of one—sort of. Regardless, this entity had such an overwhelmingly loving and grand presence that I felt the need to prostrate myself. When I asked silently, "Who are you?" I heard or felt a voice respond, "It does not matter. Please rise up, for we are all equal."

Nothing came close to that very personal, sacred communication the rest of the weekend—or ever again, for that matter. At least not one where I saw the Messenger, who delivered a message to me personally.

∞

It was my time to facilitate or teach the process, to give back what was so freely given to me. I had arrived early for the interview session with a couple of interested parties. I wasn't feeling too good either. Felt like the flu was coming on real fast. I tried to find someone to take my place, but no one was available at that late notice. I didn't have the heart to cancel because many of these people came from quite a ways, fighting LA traffic! If they were willing to go the distance, I would too—just not sit too close.

The evening was such a delight! I completely forgot about any discomfort whatsoever and proceeded to connect with them in the way which I had grown to love. However, as I said goodbye to the last one and closed the door, my head began to throb, and by the time I got home, I felt like I had been run over by a Mack truck! If only I could have held that space forever. Well, that was my goal. But obviously, I was not there yet!

∞

We were having a facilitator's meeting one night and sat in one large circle in the living room of a member's home. The process taught was always to speak from a place within, being present where Inspiration connected with reason. Now personally, I always rather liked to stay in the background when in a large group. I still had insecurities that I just couldn't shake.

However, on this particular evening, that all changed—for a while.

I remember that by some miracle, I began to offer up from that 'shared place' what I was thinking and feeling, almost from the start. What an exhilarating experience to not only tap into this space but communicate consistently from it! So, this is what it is like to live in the present. I felt so alive! Well, my evening of living in the present was short-lived. Maintaining it was...*not so easy*.

∞

A few years had flown by that were pretty glorious since that first interview, except for my marriage where we couldn't see eye to eye to make it work. Our values continued to be far too different, and with all that I had learned,

I knew that I couldn't change anyone no matter how much love you offer. It was time to go.

As I revealed before, I had lost my house. It was mortgaged to the hilt, and I would never be able to get out from underneath it alone. So, I walked away and rented a room from my dear soul sister and her husband. Another member of our community rented the last bedroom, and the four of us committed to do whatever it took to live from that 'shared place' in the heart.

It felt like we were living in a small commune. What a delight to be with people who had the same spiritual goals. It wasn't perfect; I will say that our egos were still intact, but we had a process that solved any problems that came up.

A couple more years came and went, and the energy seemed to shift within the larger community. Truth be told, I couldn't feel it like I used to. There seemed to be no forward momentum. Long story short, it was the beginning of the end. Everyone started to drift and eventually go their own way. This was all rather shocking to me, for I was sure we were creating a new movement to assist people with this process of achieving the 'shared place' where *anything* was possible!

What just happened, or better yet...why?

I had been celibate, those few years, by choice. With all that was going on or not, I decided to get my own place for a little breathing room. But my soul sister and I were going to continue to teach 'the process' to others and pick up where the founder and larger group left off. We looked at this and thought about that and just couldn't get anything off the ground. Nothing felt right! Then she became very ill.

We got into our 'shared place' and prayed, ran healing energy through her body, and others joined us from time to time...but to no avail. She was dying.

I was devastated. This woman was the second person from which I felt unconditional love! She was so amazing! How could this have happened to someone so loving, so willing to give? All on top of being able to access transformational energy that healed others.

She had assisted the community's founder through at least one major problem with his heart, where he surely would have died otherwise. For he just *knew* experientially that transformational energy would eventually prevail, making conventional medicine merely unnecessary. It was not even a choice for him anymore!

What was happening here? The unthinkable was about to enter my world at a very personal level once again. I thought a way had been found to overcome disease by transforming the physical body. All this through the eternal wellspring of Love and its healing energies, deep within the heart. Truly!

And where was God now anyway?

∞

During this present inner turmoil, I had met someone who spoke of an immense calm that had enveloped their life after taking a series of classes in Buddhism. During the graduation, a personal chant would be given individually and privately. This sounded wonderful because, quite honestly, I seemed to be spinning out of control at the time. Once more, after all I had learned and been through—I felt nowhere! So, I decided to take a slightly different path.

I loved the story of Buddha's life. I had read several books related in one way or another to his teachings. But like all religions, you have a prophet with a message that was acquired through their own personal experience, and then, when they are gone from this world, others take over, and unfortunately, changes occur.

I don't remember which particular discipline I joined. Still, I enjoyed the people and the feeling of oneness that occurred within their community, similar to the last group I was with. The actual graduation of sorts, where I was given my mantra, was quite profound in the energy it produced. It was a private affair, just the two of us. The woman began a chant that sounded like a song of different vibrations or sounds that made my hair stand on end, and finally, as my heart opened—they flew in. Then my whole system became a vortex of energy rising higher and higher, which moved me to tears. If I remember correctly, this mantra was my call to God. Wow!

However, the person that introduced me to this community needed some money and had asked quite persistently for a loan. Not just a couple of bucks either! So personal mantra or no, I was not very inclined to get involved. Anyway, the Divine experience was beautiful, but the human aspect was not so good, and I was just too raw from all that had happened in the last six months.

With my divorce behind me, the group's breakup, and my dear friend's death, it was time to make some drastic changes. I had to get away. So, I simply threw the baby out

with the bathwater! I was finished with LA, and I was finished with my quest.

Love Like No Other

A clean slate, in a new location, and I was off and running. I found work quickly. I stayed for a while with another dear friend until I could get financially stabilized, for I had arrived with only $1200.00 in my back pocket! A little wine, a little song, and dance and—okay, I can do this! Everything will be all right.

But the level of peace that I had enjoyed in the past was gone—simply gone! The pain that had settled deep inside needed to be dealt with, but apparently, I was against such action. I was running on empty. When it came to matters of the heart—the door was closed—yes, locked up real tight!

I started dating, of course, with catastrophic results, so I finally gave up. If it was meant for me to be alone, then so be it. Instead, I used my free time to focus on my art. I found someone who taught small, intimate oil painting classes in her home. Perfect! I had found a different source of fulfillment, and I didn't have to deal with men.

Six months later, one of my clients wanted to introduce me to a friend who lived in Europe but would be visiting the area. Well, I thought, you're kidding—right? I'm not interested in the least! So, thanks, but no thanks—and told her as much.

Her insistence won out, though. It was the 'dinner' aspect that sealed it. I had not had any fine dining in a while since I was going it alone; just something quick and easy to eat in front of the TV. Plus, this restaurant was new to me. It's just dinner, right? And I have always really enjoyed her and her husband's company.

I arrive at their house, and we wait for his appearance from the guest room. Then out he comes!

My first impression: handsome...but shorter and older than...it's just dinner, remember?

The food was delicious, and the company—relaxed and pleasant. Nothing memorable really, except that it just happened to be Valentine's Day, and I said yes to a second dinner, this time at their home.

Again, we had another rather pleasant experience, but no fireworks. After the meal, my friends suggested that the gentleman and I might want to take a walk outside and get some air while they cleaned up. What's with their cupid attitude anyway? But—out we went.

It was a beautiful night. Not many houses in that area of the desert were casting their light, so the stars seemed extraordinarily bright and close enough to touch. As we walked utterly alone, we felt free to talk at a more personal and intimate level. The conversation meandered, we hit upon a particular topic of great interest to me, and something began to occur within my heart. It was similar to a combination lock on a safe like in the movies.

He asks, "Do you believe in destiny?" (click)

"I have been looking for the love of my life!" (click)

There was something else mentioned about God or meditation. (another click)

With the evening over, while I was driving home, I began to feel like there *might* be something there between us to explore further. My heart was opening, but I would have to see.

The three of them came by the salon the next day, on the way to the airport, for he was going home. I suppose he was curious about where I worked. I was waiting for my next client, so I had time to chat just a bit outside. He soon left, and as I turned to enter the building, I almost ran into the glass door! In just that short span of time, he had taken my breath away!

∞

A month or so later, we arranged to meet for a couple of days, halfway between us in New York City. In my mind, this would make or break what seemed to be birthing. I had no interest in a long-distance relationship. Yes, it was all very exciting, but what was happening inside my heart influenced everything, and I was not clear about its motives. I did not feel on solid ground at all.

Upon my arrival at the hotel, he was waiting by the elevator on the fifth floor, where the lobby was located. From my lack of knowledge of big-city hotels, it was of great comfort to see him because I had no clue where to go exactly and, frankly, never heard of a lobby on any floor but the ground level!

Once ensconced in the room, I noticed a cart from room service with goodies that would sustain us as we proceeded to talk and talk some more, pausing only to change our position on the settee from which we shared our histories and dreams. Time stood still until four hours later, we began to noticed our surroundings and wondered about taking a break for dinner.

The long and short of the whole weekend encounter was beyond expectation. Well, at least for me! There were few words spoken between us in the taxi back to the airport, only a jumble of thoughts boiling down to the question of—now what? Resting my head upon his chest, I clutched his heavy winter coat with such fierceness that the knuckles of my right hand turned white. I was in a panic. Somehow during those few days together, my heart had clicked wide open! Furthermore, I allowed it to rest in someone else's hands once more! Was it safe?

∞

He had family obligations creating issues, and I had a small dog. He was in the process of selling his business, and I still had mine. He lived in Belgium, I in Arizona. There were plenty of stressors from which to feel anxious, but we managed. One thing that he said to me early on was, "If you need anything or have a problem, just let me know. I have very big shoulders!" At that moment, I experienced the truth of what he said, as it resonated deep within my heart. It was as though those shoulders and arms stretched into infinity with unconditional love. Ahhh—finally.

However, there was always that constant chatter in my head that would overshadow what I knew in my heart. I would begin to over-think things, especially around my financial situation. We were traveling a lot, and my clients were feeling the need to have someone more available. So, my business went in a downward spiral. I was an extremely independent person and was not going to ask anyone for money! I was feeling stretched real thin, almost to the breaking point. We needed to have 'the talk' soon. Decisions had to be made to take our relationship to the next level—or not.

It was challenging for me to take a stand for my needs and desires. My level of self-worth was still on the low side, and I just couldn't risk the possibility of rejection. Furthermore, I continued to stand at a distance from any spiritual guidance...by choice!

"Just a few more months," he says. Oh dear—I had heard that promise before. I felt pressed to make a decision in my best interest, so I ended the relationship. A huge leap for me, and taking it made me feel better about myself—but I missed him terribly. It was a massive shock for him. How could someone reject all that fun and excitement, jet setting around the world?

How indeed—but I had to. I mean, I felt his love, but the empty promises were saying something else!

It was not long before he made a decision that would change our lives and move us forward once again. On his next visit to Arizona, we went house hunting, and during my visit to Brussels, we found a condo. We were committed to each other and building our life together fresh.

Many of our friends in the early years would ask how we met. Every time I spoke of our relationship, I relived, or better yet, touched that wellspring of love deep down. This unconditional love feels like an embrace so gentle yet strong enough to hold me up above the fray of life, giving me respite. Remember those strong shoulders? Later on, I saw that he could hold/love me in such a way and long enough until I could learn to love myself.

∞

A little time goes by, and he is very insistent on me teaching him to meditate. It was one of the things we talked about under the stars when we first met. I felt at a loss here because how do you teach someone who is so hyper and impatient? I laughed and said, "No can do! That's impossible!" But, as is his style, he persists and persists until he gets his way.

I am reading something in a yoga pamphlet about energy this and that when a light bulb went off in my head. As I read, I saw that this was how I could explain what to do and guide him, hopefully, into his own experience of calm. I am actually excited at the prospect of being able to assist. The next morning, we begin by sitting quietly, but what happened after a few minutes came as a complete surprise! As I began to open up to my connection within, I realized how much I missed this. Tears began to flow and flow once again.

So now, I am more aware of my desire to keep my spiritual commitment upfront and center. What is my next step? Which direction would I take?

The Cosmic Field

It was the holiday season, and while on my way to Northern California to be with family, I stopped in LA to see a friend. Our lives had intersected quite a bit while on similar spiritual paths. We got caught up on the latest, and in parting, she 'paid forward' a book she had finished. The title sounded like it was straight out of my Sci-fi library!

Once I started, though, there was so much that spoke to me. I felt compelled to underline almost the entire book. It was my second introduction to *A Course In Miracles*. But instead of these concepts flying over my head, they began to take root and left me wanting more. I broke out the original set of books I had bought years ago that comprise the complete *Course* and started at the beginning. Within six months, I had my first out of body experience, where I was aware of reading at the table but watching myself doing so.

The next experience was a real hair-raiser! I was at the same table early in the morning, during my quiet time of study and contemplation, when all of a sudden, I found myself in a place of darkness that was absolute. There was nothing else. Needless to say, I was terrified. But as the tears ran down my cheeks, I extended that experience by relaxing as best I could and found myself whispering, "I'm okay...it's all right..." to myself or whomever.

I felt I had no one to talk to for clarification on such matters except maybe...

∞

I started calling members of the last group in LA that I had spent the six years with, at least the few I could find. No one knew of the founder's whereabouts or what had happened to him. Now, why did I not try to locate someone who studied and taught the *Course*? I really don't know. I just felt a strong impulse to talk with the founder instead because he had provided multiple experiences that had moved me beyond compare.

Time was going by as it always does; I was getting impatient, so I tried the good 'ole operator, and voila, there he was! It was just way too simple. I called him and made a rendezvous for a couple of months out when I would be driving through alone on my way to see the family for Christmas. I wanted an 'in-person' discussion about my recent experiences.

∞

Upon arrival at his place, we spent at least four hours discussing everything from A to Z. Nothing had occurred in those four hours that was expected. Nothing. When you sit with a powerful mystic, the only thing you can expect is the unexpected. In fact, not until I went outside to get something in the car did I realize how expanded I felt. Even a bit lightheaded, but I could sense my field of energy start to shrink back into my physical body in no time as I walked. I kid you not!

His response to the experience of finding myself in complete and total darkness was, "It is not supposed to be scary!" Yeah, as if!

The next morning, I am on the road with my Starbucks, and just about 45 minutes into the drive, I find myself cresting the mountains, entering the flatlands. I reflected on my visit the day before and wondered if I was up to being involved once more with this person. He had asked if I felt moved to join with him and others, living a fully connected life of Inspiration. He said that we are interconnected (like a vast computer network) by Cosmic Forces or 'Energy' stretching into Infinity/Reality/God as One Mind. Mankind could and would benefit from the counsel of this Intelligence, which is greater than our own—via Inspiration or that 'ah-ha' moment.

Still driving, my mind had wandered into the possibilities when a rather bold Vision flashed before me in my mind's eye. The view through the windshield opened up into this indescribable, gorgeous panorama, reminding me of the previously said interconnectedness but in spectacular color! I felt then and there that this Vision was a direct signal to begin the next leg of my spiritual path with this modern-day mystic.

∞

I ended up putting my study of the *Course* on hold while I began to work with him, doing what I could to help publish his book and make a re-emergence into the public with his message.

One of my more unusual experiences of Cosmic Energy was very healing. Honestly, I had been experiencing this Energy more often than not all along, but now my awareness of it seemed more precise and much more expanded!

One night, in my dream, I felt a severe earthquake which opened a split in the floor on which I was standing. The floor tilted towards that crevasse, but instead of falling, I shot straight up like a comet! As I was flying through space, I could look down and see my body lying in bed. In what was probably only seconds, I came back into my body and fell asleep.

Upon awakening, I remembered every detail. And boy, did I feel good! I had been suffering from pain in my hips and had to wear good support shoes to walk any distance. But after my cosmic sojourn, I was as limber as a young, Olympic gymnast! Sadly, it didn't last but 36 hours or so. But—I do not suffer from joint pain anymore.

No explanation was forthcoming! It just simply happened.

∞

Much later on, a red spot the size of a dime appeared on my temple. I thought nothing of it. It itched a little, leading me to believe it was just a rash of some sort. No big deal!

Well—that spot, over a period of a couple of weeks, grew down my face and onto my cheek. Still, nothing to get nervous about. However, it eventually dropped down to my neck then began to move over to my left side and up to cover my entire neck and face! Up to this point, other than being unsightly, it just itched a lot. I had bought every ointment known to civilization to try to alleviate this itch plus the heat that had begun to accompany it—all to no avail!

Finally, I broke. I couldn't sleep at all one night. I applied everything I had bought thus far all at once. I even put ice packs on for brief periods. The experience was unbearable. I wanted to use my hairbrush and rip the skin right off my face! When I looked in the mirror, the redness had moved up to my lower eyelids. I had no idea if this malady would affect my eyesight or not, but I certainly didn't want to take that chance. I got up that morning and went to the emergency because, naturally, it was now Sunday.

I normally don't see doctors. In fact, I don't have medical insurance because I use the Cosmic Energy for healing if it gets to that point. My lack of faith cost me $1000.00 cash and whatever the cost of the prescription I was given. I was told that it was topical dermatitis and that I most likely was allergic to something I put on my face. Yeah, whatever...

Where did my trust in the Energy go? Right out the window, I'm afraid!

In retrospect, that night was most likely the worst of it. After discussing my experience with the mystic I'd been intensely working with, it felt right that I had been rapidly processing through all the toxic thoughts or beliefs I had gathered this lifetime. And I simply couldn't move it out of my system fast enough!

Slowly, sheet upon sheet of skin began to peel off. What was left was new, smooth, and fresh as a baby's skin. Hmmm—symbolic???

∞

A few years later, I developed a bladder infection out of the blue! It went from bad to worse. I could not urinate but a few drops of blood, and the pain was again unbearable! It occurred on a Sunday like before (was this a test?) but I nevertheless began to panic once more. Pain will do that. But I also knew at some level that I could heal this problem.

So, I'm sitting on the toilet and talking to the affected area. I am literally saying, "I don't need this, I don't want this, and it—will—stop—now!" The pain dissipated, and I was finally able to do my business. Now, mind you, it did come back a couple of days later. The situation was not as intense, but I repeated what I stated before with the same results. I knew at that moment I would be successful in my healing. There is trust, faith, and optimism, but nothing compares to knowing that I am part of a greater Intelligence at work. And I knew that this Intelligence could be called on anytime for anything, but sadly, I would forget.

Six years flew by. They were difficult as well as exhilarating. This mystic was brilliant and expected only excellence from those he worked with. As a result, I had grown more during that time than all the years combined since *The Shock*. But it was definitely, hard on the relationship with my partner. I believe he was jealous—not only of the man but the time and energy I put into the project, for he had not a clue what it was about. We had talked and talked about the invisible world, but he never really understood. I, on the other hand, just wanted off this rock, never to return!

It was painful knowing that both relationships were right for me and feeling like I had to choose between the two. The discord in my love relationship had become unbearable and a difficult distraction when working with the other. Had I outgrown the relationship with my partner? We had even separated for a while.

But, as it finally turned out, the mystic had outgrown me! No matter what, we just couldn't move the message forward. The Cosmic Hand seemed motionless in that regard, for whatever reason. We went our own way. However, it took me months to recover from what felt like a betrayal of sorts. I had bent over backwards and jumped through hoops for him—for a Cosmic Cause! It was heart-wrenching. Something apparently was blocked, or everything would have blossomed and brought this Cosmic Vision to fruition. All I ever wanted was to be part of something bigger than myself, to help mankind find a way out of the chaos of fear and pain.

I began to live in a more secular fashion once again.

BUT what was my purpose? Why was I here on this planet? I couldn't make any sense of it all.

The Course

When the void in my heart began to grow, I became motivated to move forward on my spiritual journey—again. I picked up *A Course In Miracles* and started at the beginning.

Suffice it to say, I must have been ready to study and spend the much-needed time with myself. I would generally get up at least an hour earlier than my partner and do just that! It took me over a year to do the 365 Lessons, study the Text and just sit quietly. When he played golf, I took advantage of the extra time (sometimes all 4 hours), believe it or not, for it was that satisfying!

∞

One experience that stands out during this time reinforced what is written in the *Course* in many different ways but basically saying that what we do to our brother, we do to ourselves for we are One. Now, as I reread this last sentence, it is saying a lot. However, I don't want to get into the details but simply stick to my experiences.

I don't remember the circumstances exactly, except that my face, more so than my body, flashed over the person's face in front of me. It was a bit startling, but that was it! I saw my image long enough (seconds most likely) to recognize that Truth.

∞

This next one came in the form of a dream. An authentic feeling dream—like I was living it.

I am at a reunion of sorts. I hooked up with a stranger who knew precisely what she wanted. I found myself riding shotgun with her. I didn't know where we were, but I was feeling very excited. When I chose to ride along, I thought it would be a simple weekend getaway. We picked up a few other people here and there that I didn't know. I ask where we were going, and she points to the gorgeous mountains straight ahead. "See that tallest peak; that is where we are headed. Those are the Himalayas!" she said with reverence and joy.

"OMG...that's the other side of the world!" I retort as she smiled.

We stop and make camp, but there are precious little supplies for food, and for some reason, it seems like we will be staying for a while. I walk into a room that has a small cookstove with one pot sitting on top. A stew of some sort was heating, but as I looked closer, there was a catsup bottle half submerged. Obviously, there was not much to eat at all.

Another girl walks in and notices the catsup bottle sticking up and casually comments that it looked yummy. Then the woman who is in charge turned to me and asked about my purse. I froze. "What's this?" she asks even though she knew full well.

I gasp! Because it is not the purple purse I care about, but what is inside. I hand over the purse, and she pulls out a single piece of paper. On it is a list of all my accomplishments and, yes, even a photo of myself. I smile as I reach for it and caress the image one last time.

I put it in her hands, oh so tenderly, and watched as she dropped it into the soup.

I had just chosen to let *everything* I valued—go.

∞

Are you still with me? LOL.

Well, it's a dream after all, but the fact that it was so long, detailed, and full of symbolism true to the *Course*, I was inspired to include it as an essential part of my journey. I had written it all down when I woke, not to forget anything! And the dream is a perfect setup for the next event.

The Walls Came Tumbling Down

By now, I have a very easy, natural relationship with the Voice—as I call It. I am leaving the health food store when my head turns towards a magazine stand with different periodicals offered free to the public. The rack was in the opposite direction of where I was headed, but I felt the pull. Usually, I am no longer interested in what they have to offer since it is mostly articles about natural living with metaphysical articles and ads. Been there and done that, decades ago! But I pick up the one that I was *supposed* to and shoved it in with the groceries.

At home, it is thrown on a heap of other material to read at some point. Weeks later, my interest is peaked, and I opened it up. I scan every single article and advertisement, looking for what? I don't know. Finally, next to the last page, I see it—a one by two-inch ad about writing a best seller in one weekend. I admitted to myself that the statement seemed preposterous! I went online to the website and checked it out—thoroughly.

The author/mentor spoke about releasing the Divine author within through direct union with God—which was right up my alley. He offered complimentary evening work-shops to give people a firsthand experience. The next one was offered in Sedona—one of my favorite places on the planet and only a two-hour drive. Now, I need to share this Inspiration and my desire to attend the retreat with my partner.

"You don't need to do this! Haven't you done enough?" he says.

"This seems different, though. I would simply love to feel free enough to be able to write or paint with abandon and not with an internal critic!" Tears are forming as I fully immerse myself in the moment with that critic—creating a tinge of despair. "Let's go and make a fun trip of it. Besides, it's free!"

He relented, and I reserved a seat for one while he would stay at the hotel.

The two hours went by fast. The methodology used was potent, or I was ready, or both, but the experience produced, was startling enough to know this was indeed my next step. I was about to enter into an adventure that would explore the 'stars in my heart' with God and my younger self at around five years of age. Well, that's what came to me that evening, with enough power to move mountains.

∞

It was a three-day, two night intensive at a hotel with meals included. Without a lot of boring details, I can say this: I could not write as instructed. There was no flow of words coming from the Divine place within. I produced only gibberish! Nice!

However, I did have several *experiences*. It seems that I functioned differently than most of the others. Also, I did notice for the first time that my brain is dyslexic. Reason or excuse—don't know. But most likely, probably why I hated school!

Friday night goes by with nothing to show. Saturday morning, it is suggested that we all ask within what the title of the book we are writing will be. What occurred happened so fast and precise that I had no opportunity to think about the fact that there was no book forthcoming—as yet! The title was, *The Walls Came Tumbling Down*. I was very moved by this experience and knew it to be authentic. (But as a side note—it came to be that the title had already been taken. Thus, it is the title for this section only, and an endnote experience, soon to be revealed, of a lifelong quest.)

I kept struggling, so after lunch, I spoke with the instructor. I state that I must be blocked entirely and would simply go home rather than torture myself any further. Now, there is a red flag!!! Running away has always been a favorite MO for me.

He tells me to be patient, and if I felt moved, I could work with one of the assistants to see what was what. I give myself another hour, even went to my room for a breather. I come back and decide to give it one hundred percent. What did I have to lose? And I certainly wasn't going to get a refund!

I located the assistant and told her I must be blocked. She was pleased to help. She had me go into the hallway to a small couch where we would have some privacy, and I was to lie down and relax. Well, that was impossible! I was too fearful of getting prone and way too nervous about getting any measure of being comfortable. So, with my arms over my face and my legs bent up as far as they could go facing the back of the couch—I waited in misery.

She's sitting in a chair right next to me, noticed my posture, and asked a couple of questions. Then held up a crystal pendulum over a book as I'm screaming (in my mind) that; *I don't believe in this, it is ridiculous, and I am out of here!* She is praying very quickly but softly for the privacy factor, and

I can barely understand a word. I did hear her calling on an Angel, don't remember which one *(this isn't happening!!!)*, and something about times when we are/play the victim and other times when we are/play the victimizer.

Something shifted inside my system, and an indescribable peace washed over me. I completely relaxed. My legs slid down, my arms went to my side, and I felt like I was floating. She was done. I was to stay put until I felt ready to continue writing.

WRITE! How is that possible? I just want to bask in this glorious space. I am no longer wounded. I feel pristine, free at last from any negativity, hurt, or fear. Total bliss! WOW!

That is why the little girl in me appeared at the complimentary evening, weeks prior, encouraging me to do this intensive. Interesting... And what is more interesting is the fact that I have covered this childhood issue a thousand times already using different methodologies. Well—looks like the walls did indeed come tumbling down!

∞

I don't know how I will manage to sit and write. Because all I want to do is stand and beam all this light—my light—that came from deep inside!

Eventually, though, I do sit and what occurs next is the Vision that I wrote about at the beginning of the book called *Smoke and Mirrors*.

That Vision was like a scene out of a movie, and I could just imagine a director saying, "CUT!" The scene was over. No one or anything was needed anymore! Done.

I am stunned by this Revelation! Because I now know that life is like a movie—all props! The planet is a prop, and the body is a prop, all to support the director's story—and the director is me! This life of mine is my story written by me *and* can be changed by me anytime! I am in full control!

∞

I just want to go home and digest it all. The rest of the weekend, which wasn't much, flew by. As I left, I paid the assistant who did the crystal thingy and said that she did indeed unblock me and I was eternally grateful. Big hug, big kiss!

I drove home, higher than a kite—infinitely higher!

I did lose some altitude, though, when my partner did not understand why I didn't come home with a manuscript for the book I had intended to write! All that time and money down the drain?!!

He calmed down as I began to put my notes together from the retreat and commenced to write. My heart soared once more reliving those experiences and all the previous ones, as I started from the very beginning of my quest some 40 years ago.

∞

I could not finish until now, a little over three years later.

My partner opted for open-heart surgery since he could not exert himself at all without being short of breath.

Without his guidance from the Higher Intelligence on the matter, or even adhering to the doctor's advice afterward, it did not go well—at all.

Without going into detail, those three years for me became caretaking years. It was a sad, exhausting, and even frustrating time, as his physical and, more importantly, mental state deteriorated. It seemed like the more he felt less than his prior self, the more fear and anger came to the forefront. After wrestling with his demons, day and night, it soon felt like I had nothing left to give. Even though I could and did connect to the Higher Intelligence I had experienced, it didn't take much to lose that connection. I simply couldn't continue. What a drama!!!

And on top of all that, I felt even more sadness, pain, and guilt over the decision to stop taking care of him. I considered extensively the basis of our relationship, which had always been the wellspring of our love, my commitment to that love—and to him.

As I searched for a decision that would bring me peace and joy once again, I began to realize that it was not the loving spirit that's him I was leaving, but his ego. I felt better but not completely free.

He is in Belgium, and I am home finishing my story.

∞

This morning (real-time), I was lying in bed, waking up slowly and letting my mind wander. I don't remember specific thoughts, but you can bet that they were related to this relationship.

I then felt my system or mind expand as an experience settled in. I saw my part in the chaos of emotions within the relationship. I felt what it was like to enable someone's darkness. Once again—I could no longer be a victim. In fact, not ever—under any circumstance!

As the days progressed, I saw how I was an enabler in all my relationships from the get-go, especially the people I loved that were strong-willed. For the most part, I am now able to energetically embrace my partner of 20 years in my thoughts with unconditional love. No regrets, no wanting anything to be different, no emotions to muddy the ebb and flow of Love's grace within my heart. I can see that our 'gifts' were/are perfect for each other. Even our shortcomings and especially our shortcomings, for they were an opportunity to see them for what they were, let them go, allowing Love's Presence within to shine.

In fact, it is my intent, moving forward, to energetically embrace everyone with Love. An example, just the other day (during crazy COVID), a lady called me an a$$ hole as we approached each other, still twelve feet apart. I had taken off my mask after exiting the store, which horrified her—I guess. I apologized and commented that we were still outside of the 'danger zone' when she again called me the same, delicate name! I certainly wasn't thrilled, to say the least, but I chose to send her loving energy instead of picking a fight over who was right! After all, I didn't know any of the burdens or fears she carried in her heart. And she didn't know that I wear a mask only for the 'comfort' of others. I don't feel the need for myself.

To be honest, I had to repeat my prayer and visualization several times until the hurt vanished, and the whole scenario seemed comical! We are such silly creatures; soooo much to fight about!

I know that as I continue to live this way, I will be opening doors, inviting Love to Be, and things will change—for the better—for the world. I cannot limit myself or my brother, for then I would be limiting God.

As quoted from the *Course*, "Forgiveness paints a picture of a world where suffering is over, loss becomes impossible and anger makes no sense. Attack is gone and madness has an end. The world becomes a place of Joy, abundance, charity, and endless giving. It is now so like Heaven that it quickly is transformed into the Light that it reflects."

Conclusion(s)

So, what is Love? Love is what we are.

Can we really love someone more than another? No, I would call that need or attachment. Perhaps, a strong bond comes from being together in other lifetimes/dreams. I feel like that is not only possible but likely.

I am blessed to have experienced unconditional love. I believe that that feeling is a precursor in this physical world for the Love God has for us—but only as a pale version of it.

All of my experiences have involved the invisible world. So, that right there proves to me that there is so much more than meets the physical eye. The entities, the cosmic/healing Energy, and all the Visions presented at just the right time to take me to the next level of spiritual advancement; eliminating the blocks to Love. Love of myself, my brothers and sisters, and of course, our Creator. Plus, awakening from the dream and knowing that we are all One Eternal Son created from the Mind of God.

∞

Now, how does one talk about God when words can't come close to expressing what is from infinite silence?

Well, I will try anyway within the parameters of my personal perspective.

I believe in God, our Father/Creator. God is perfect—period.

Being alone, I believe He wanted to share "the wealth of His Being" (a quote from the mystic). This desire or thought was like a Big Bang, which brought about the creation of us, His Son, in His own image of perfect Love, Light, and Wisdom—as one vast Mind. At some point, part of the Son had a thought that took him outside of Perfection.

The instant this occurred, God put in place a connection, from His sleeping Son back to Him, while the Son dreamed of being something else, somewhere else. One might call that connection the Holy Spirit, the Cosmic Hand, the Voice, the Silver Thread, and so on and so forth. I just know that help is always present.

Earth was created in the heavens (probably from a second Big Bang) and evolved enough to house life so that consciousness could also evolve to the point of Self-discovery. This is purely speculation on my part but does make sense to me. After having stated this, it does bring to my attention a memory of another Vision I had when I was working with the mystic years back.

∞

I had been discussing over dinner the topic of God, Creation, the Garden of Eden, etc., with my partner, who's a Catholic Christian, and sharing what I thought was true.

I realized then that I was stumped as to exactly when consciousness had taken on the human form, and I could not respond from a knowing place within me.

So, I am lying in bed that night wide awake. I noticed that it was 2:00 AM as I reviewed what he had stated about Adam and Eve. I had responded at the time that I absolutely knew that God did not gently set the lovely couple down in the Garden of Eden. However, I also did not believe that humanity's roots had evolved from single-celled organisms or life forms that crawled out of the vaporous waters either. Or did it?

So, I began to wonder about which upright, bipedal creatures had become the first recipients of consciousness and then, of course, when. Shortly after that, I began to spontaneously experience a condensed, visual montage of the evolutionary process of our physical world—all playing out in my mind. It was as though my consciousness had opened up and expanded out, having a direct connection with a greater Intelligence outside of myself once again.

First, I experienced that we humans in our original, invisible state created from and by Almighty God; have a greater connected consciousness as one, vast Mind. In *my* mind, I saw this vast Mind, with its infinite capabilities, begin to create the world of matter.

There was no specific time or event that life occurred but rather a gradual evolution like a natural selection until consciousness finally became conscious of itself as an individualized physical entity. The next step was to develop or discover its conscience or perhaps the desire to do right instead of only survive.

So, in answer to the Creation/Evolution quandary, I saw that they both were involved. Our world of matter was created instantly, but then a seemingly slow evolutionary process began to unfold. Again, it seemed like a continuous, grand experiment with the ultimate purpose being—Self-discovery. What are we?

It is obvious that what we have manifested is not in harmony. Since harmony is a direct inheritance from God, it seems to me that perhaps finding harmony/Love through existence is our primary directive.

And I think it is safe to assume that it may be the 'sleeping mind' that had a need for creating the physical world, or—God did, solely for man to find his way back Home.

The greatest impression I walked away with is the shift in my perspective that we *are* all One, acting as one. Our actions and reactions not only affect others but ourselves simultaneously.

On the heels of that experience (all of this happening within a four-hour time frame), I found myself traveling far enough out into Infinity to be able to see this vast Mind working as a System in the world of matter. This was not a dream, for I was aware of my physical body in bed while also viewing this System below me.

From this perspective, I am experiencing freedom like none other. Interestingly, I found myself inhaling the pure 'space' in which I found myself while simultaneously feeling my physical chest rise and fall in unison. I simply wanted to absorb as much as possible—if possible.

I imagine that this experience is akin to the experience of dying and leaving the physical body. I simply went much further. Maybe...

∞

So, why would we leave our state of Perfection? Did we have a desire to be God, rather than being content with *'of like Mind'* with God? If true, I believe; first it would be impossible, wanting or trying to be something else. It simply wouldn't work because you can't change Perfection, or it would no longer be perfect. Second, God would not allow Himself to be separated from a part of Himself as His perfect Creations. And thank goodness, or we would be doomed forever.

Perhaps, there was fear involved after that initial wayward thought—which brought on the dreams of escape—trying to hide from guilt or retribution??? Who knows!!!

All I know is that we can wake up! And all of this conflict will disappear like it never happened.

∞

I'm going to change it up a bit and talk about Jesus now. Perfect timing since tonight is Christmas Eve.

I believe He is a Brother. Of course, part of God's Son with us.

Now, did He have a thought outside of Perfection as we did, or did He volunteer, so to speak, to enter the physical world and show us the Truth? I don't know.

I do know this; He overcame any and all ego that presented itself while in the physical body, stayed true to Himself and what He had experienced or knew as Truth. And then knowingly walked into a situation only to be tortured and then crucified for us/mankind, all to prove that we are not the physical body but existing Eternally with our Father/Creator.

He demonstrated Love. He demonstrated healing, knowing He was connected to God's Infinite Intelligence as God's Son. And He demonstrated forgiveness, which is the ability to see beyond the ego and this temporary, physical world of dreams.

I cannot love Him more as I write those words.

He also dictated *A Course In Miracles* for us.

I sit in gratitude.

A Few Favorite Quotes By Jesus From
A Course In Miracles

"There is nothing about me that you cannot attain. I have nothing that does not come from God. The main difference between us as yet, is that I have nothing else."

"The holiest of all the spots on earth is where an ancient hatred has become a present love...And all the lights in Heaven grow brighter, in gratitude for what has been restored."

"You are wholly lovely. A perfect shaft of pure light. Before your loveliness the stars stand transfixed and bow to the power of your will. You were created above the angels because your role involves creation as well as protection. You who are in the image of the Father need bow only to Him, before whom I kneel with you."

Amen...

CPSIA information can be obtained
at www.ICGtesting.com
Printed in the USA
LVHW070723020321
680248LV00013B/848